# 50K+ Blog Views

Learn from a man who did it on how to get
50,000+ views on your first blog

Ahemad R Kazi

# Table of Contents

# Introduction

*"We must not only blog what is popular, we must blog about our passions, no matter how quaint. This is true empowerment"*

–Su_Layug

Have you ever thought about writing a blog? Do you know what a blog is? DO you know how to make some crazy money from your blog? Let me "the man who did it" tell you that YES!! It is possible. You can create a blog for free and still make a decent amount of money doing that.

In this book, I will unlock the secrets of how I started my first blog and how I took that first blog to get 50,000+ views in less than 7 months. Writing a blog is easy. If a young student with no background in writing like me could do it, trust me – you can too.

Take this book as a step-by-step handbook to your dreams and apply the teachings as soon as possible because as I said – **IT IS FREE!!!** This is a beginner to advance guide.

No spam, no copy, no just talk, I am writing from my own experience, and it is better to learn from someone who did it than from a random and artificial guru who read about it somewhere and is now throwing that knowledge at you blindly. I am telling you that if you do exactly what I teach in the remaining book, you can make 50,000+ views and even more if you want to.

So, are you guys ready to go out there and make an impact through nothing more than your writing skills? Say HELL YEAH!!!

In this book, I will tell you

1) What is a blog and why you need it?
2)  How to start your first blog?
3) What do you need to start?
4) How you should write?
5) Tips and tricks
6) SEO tips
7) How to get 50K+ views
8) What not to do while writing a blog?
9) Why do most people fail?
10) How to monetize? Different ways to monetize!
11) And much, much, much more…

BEFORE going to the actual part, let me walk you through a disclaimer.

# *Disclaimer*

The results are not typical. It doesn't mean that you will read this book and you will get 50,000 views out of the blue. Let me tell you straight forward instead of keeping you in dark that more than 90% of the people reading this won't even start a blog and hence won't reach any other LEVEL.

There is work involved. And not just a little work, know that.

But yes, if you are serious about doing something in your life and making an impact on thousands of people with persistence and dedication, then I can surely tell you that the title of this book is going to be your **daily target**...BELIEVE THAT.

Without further ado, let's get into it!

# Chapter 1:

## *What and Why Blog?*

*"Blogging is just writing using a particularly efficient type of publishing technology"*

–Simon Dumenco

Before jumping to the advanced stuff, let me tell you about what a blog is and why you need a blog?

You see, a blog is a one-page website or landing page on which you upload the information that you want people around the world to know. It could be a helpful thing to have if you are an individual doing it as a side gig, sharing your knowledge, promoting your business, or building credibility.

People who read your blog know that you are not a fake personality and you are serious about your business and brand. It is a good way to make people believe you. You even create a fan base if people love what you write.

Many times, if you have visited any website, on the header across the menu bar along-side home, service, etc. you must have seen a tab called "BLOG". Isn't it?

When you click on that tab, it takes you to the blog of that individual or company. On that blog, they give their information, referrals, and even free stuff to hook you in. So, have you ever thought about why these people have that? Yes, there can be multiple reasons such as

1)Growing business.

2)Getting exposure and fame.

3)Building value and credibility.

4)Making decent money and much more.

And from my own personal experience, I can say that a blog is a very easy and helpful way to do all the things listed above in a well-dignified manner. Whenever you write with the sole intention of providing value, you get positive feedback, which turns into popularity, later fame, and eventually MONEY.

## Passive Income Through Blog

A blog can help you generate passive income and build a reputation for yourself and your work. Let me explain to you in a way you will understand. See the diagram below and make it clear how the cycle goes.

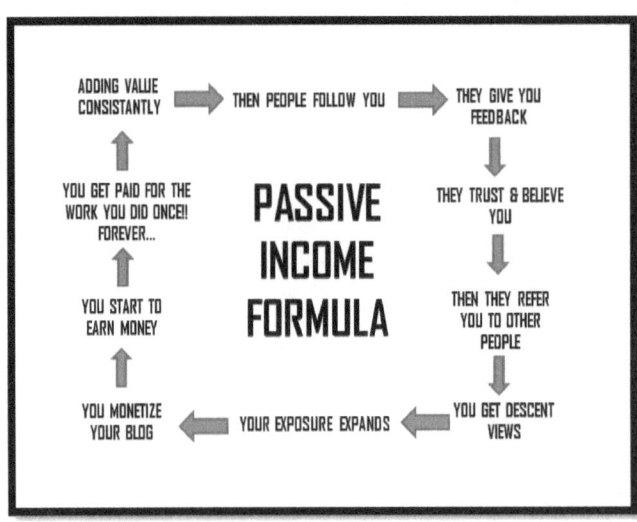

If you are looking to start a blog in order to make a quick buck then don't bother. The blogging sector is for people looking to add value to somebody's life. Making money is a definite outcome but not the end goal. The only way you can rise to the top of this game is if you are willing to take a long shot.

You will have to endure through the rough times where there will be no views to your precious blog post. You will spend hours on the screen refreshing to see some views just to get disappointed. During these times, your mind will tell you to quit and find something else that works.

Just like me, when you are hit with self-doubt; wait for a moment and ask yourself: *Did I really put in all that hard work just to call it quits?* Answer yourself and keep going. Pick a topic, create content, and publish it on your blog.

After a long wait and many cuts and bruises, you will finally be recognized by a small group of individuals. These people will find you because you were adding value consistently. They like what you are doing and as a token of appreciation, they will follow you on social media platforms.

They will come back and read your blog posts. They will share it with their friends and family members. They will even provide you honest feedback down in the comments section. You may not believe it but you are making a fan club.

I strongly suggest you take the feedback with a positive attitude; this character will take you a long way. If people tell you to improve in a certain section then that doesn't mean that they are criticizing your art, it means that they want you to become better.

After they provide you with honest feedback and stick around to see your next move, it means that they now trust you and certainly believe in you. Keep that in mind and make the changes accordingly to grow and eventually grow better.

Always remember that your readers are everything and you must listen to them and not yourself. Of course, do what you love but do not get egoistic and ignore your readers. When you listen to your audience, they can make it out and they will hold you worthy of their time.

This will increase your exposure and make your audiences wider. When many people read and like your content, you automatically get the views you were hoping for.

Now comes the best part. When you track and witness that you are getting a decent amount of views and comments you can now go ahead and monetize your blog which is the other reason you started to write.

As time passes, you will see that you are making a living out of it provided that your content is amazing. And you know what thrilled me the first time I came across this concept? That I only have to create the content once and leave it out on the internet to show me it's magic. It creates cash flow literally FOREVER!!! Isn't that phenomenal?

I mean who the hell pays you for the job you did once? Nobody. That is the power of writing a blog. Did you see how influential this model is to create a passive income? With this, don't you think you will get everything you ever need and desire? Absolutely!

Now that you are aware of this power, are you ready to create a blog for yourself and make an impact? Let's begin.

# Chapter 2:

## *Starting A Blog*

*"A blog is only as interesting as the interest shown in others"*

–Lee Oden

There are many ways in which you can start writing a blog. If you understand the coding languages like html, css, javascript, etc. then you can build a personalized blog for yourself. But if you have no clue about coding and find it boring like me, then do not break a sweat.

Due to the advancement of technology, you too could build a stunning website in a matter of hours and start your blogging career within a day. Many platforms provide an easy way out. There are multiple platforms you can use to create your first blog such as:

1) www.blogger.com/
2) www.wix.com/
3) www.wordpress.org/

Even though I started from blogger.com which is an official blogging platform from Google, I highly recommend you to start your career using WordPress. I cannot recommend them enough. WordPress is an incredible and easy solution for non-techies. They provide 1000's of free templates which you can install in seconds and build your website. You will be amazed at how easy it is.

A piece of advice, if you are not sure about this path and are not looking to spend any money then you can choose www.blogger.com. Google allows you to create your blog for free on this platform.

The only downside is that you won't have your own personalized domain name like www.yourdomain.com. Instead, you will get something like blogger.com/yourdomain which is not at all professional. Blogger.com also provides you with proper exposure through the webmaster tools on which we will talk later.

I created my first blog from blogger.com and I did well, I guess. So, if you don't want to spend money then go for the blogger.com

But before going to the creation part, there are a series of tasks that you need to handle. Follow these steps and answer the questions. I suggest that you write down the answers to the following questions, this will help you get clarity and inspire you to go through with it.

Questions:

1) Why do you want to start a blog?

2) What are you trying to accomplish through your blog?

3) Are you willing to put in the effort and stay persistent?

4) Will you get discouraged if it doesn't get a lot of what you expect?

5) Will you try your best to reach the top?

Until and unless you don't have the answers to these questions, I suggest you don't begin. Period. Until you have the answer to the why? The how will not come to you.

These are very important questions and they are meant to align the mindset that can motivate you during tough times.

Many people started blogs and only a handful of them succeeded. So, I will not say that you can easily succeed, I would be a liar if I say so, but if you do what is mandatory, then you can succeed. Once you have the answers to the above questions and you are fully convinced that you want to start no matter what, then let me tell you how you could do it despite the odds being stacked against you.

The most important thing about starting a blog is **FINDING A NICHE.** Yes! you must find a particular area which you can talk about and provide information and value. You must know that you can either be the first one or you can be the best one in that particular niche to make an impact and fulfill your dreams.

Let me warn you that the path you are paving for yourself will be rough and there are a few things you must consider and always keep in mind. Write this down and paste it on the wall in front of you.

### 1)Write Your Passion:

Find a niche that you can be most passionate about and can write for a long time even if no one is watching or reading your blog. That could be a key to success. If you are writing about something that you love to talk about then you can go on and on. That is when you can provide the most value.

And the time will eventually come when you will find the right type of passionate audience that will read your posts and follow you and push you into the "passive income formula" cycle.

Most people start writing a blog on a topic they have no idea about. Just because people are liking that stuff and it is in trend, does not mean that you should start writing that. This is one of the reasons why you could fail miserably.

## 2)Be Consistent:

Even if you have a good topic to cover and you know plenty of things about it, does not mean that you can post one blog in 3 months or once in six months or once a year. That much delay could ruin your exposure and people will forget who you are. There are thousands of bloggers out there, you don't want to lose to them.

You should fix a particular time period in which you can post and make the habit of publishing your posts at the time you have committed.

Many people post daily, some post weekly and some even do it monthly. That is completely up to you. Whatever time frame you decide, stick to it till the end, and don't miss out. I used to post weekly. Every Sunday I used to post and used to get a good response.

According to me, one week is a good time period because people don't forget you that fast if they liked your blog and it gives time for your blog to rank in the search and attract more audiences to your posts.

Again, whatever you chose, stick to it consistently.

### 3)Embrace Failure:

This is the quality of millionaires and billionaires that you could develop through blogging. Whenever a post doesn't do that good and if you receive some negative comments and feedback; doesn't mean that you should give up and stop doing your part.

It was discovered that **the one who embrace failures and still goes on – succeeds.** I believe that success lies on the other side of failure. So, until you are not failing, you are not growing.

### 4)Grow Every Day:

The most important thing you need to do is growing every day. Your second post must be better than your first and your third must be better than your second one in some way or other. So, that one day when you have posted your say $200^{th}$ post, and when you go back to see your $1^{st}$ one, you just smile and say "**Thank God I grew.**"

When you concentrate on growing rather than the money or fame, believe me, that your prize will be even greater and honorable.

### 5)Change accordingly:

Never be scared of doing everything again. When you have written a blog post and if in the end, you are not sure if it will work or not, then do not hesitate to make changes. Be

13

your own critic and have the courage to say that "**I made a mistake**" this will only strengthen you and make you better in the long term.

When you are posting once in a week, it is not that every-time you write a post, it will come up to be the perfect one. It won't. You have 6 days to make your post an attractive piece of art.

You must have to change many things, tweak a little here and little there, and sometimes you can even have to write everything from scratch. Don't hesitate and say that I am done and POST it anyway. Take time and that time will be worth it...

After gaining the insights and knowing all that; you must now know exactly what you must do. There are many sections that come into considerations. But don't worry, I will walk you through each and every one of them and explain to you in the simplest terms possible.

# Chapter 3:

## *How to Begin?*

*"Blogging is like work, but without co-workers thwarting you at every turn"*

–Scott Adams

After you are convinced and confident about yourself then you should start immediately. At this point, you will have a niche to provide information about. You can choose any niche like technology, fitness, health, food, games, educational, tutorial, and many more.

There are millions and millions of topics in the world to select from. But make sure to narrow your niche to the most bottom, because when you do that, you can target only that particular audience and will eventually make an impact.

Now you may ask what does narrowing down means? Well, a good question. See technology is a huge topic. There are so many sections and variations, and in the confusion of all that people are bewildered about why to stay at your blog when they can get the same from someone else.

Narrowing down means that instead of going for the technology topic, go for the mobile, or a particular mobile brand, a particular brand of laptop, and just one thing. This shows that you will write about only one mobile brand and now that is narrowing. For instance, instead of picking the topic like books, select the topic as self-help books or go deeper and select a subsection under that.

By this, people can know and say that *oh yeah, he does this and writes about this only, he must be knowing many things about that sector and he must be an expert.* BOOM! Just like that, you are now an expert in your field. Awesome!

My topic was "luxury cars and technology" and it was a huge topic so I decided to narrow it down to one particular car and that was ROLLS ROYCE! A perfect combination of luxury mixed with the latest technology.

My blog was about Rolls Royce cars, so people who are looking for information about Rolls Royce could lend on my blog any-time. That could be an absolute example of narrowing your niche. Now that you have decided your niche, it's time to go to the next step...

# Chapter 4:

## *Branding*

*"Don't focus on having a great blog. Focus on producing a blog that's great for your readers"*

–Brian Clark

You have a topic, now it is time to give your blog a cool and attractive name that people can click on as soon as they find it on the internet. You have to take your time on this because this name will become your identity. You don't want to be stuck with a lame name.

It is not something that could be done hastily. See, good branding leads to a better attraction and exposure. You surely don't want to keep your brand a lowly thing that is another name for diapers, do you?

So, take your own sweet time and do some research on unique words. Now you don't have to create your own words, but yes surely you must find something unique.

When you are good, you could be better and best but when you are unique you are unique – nothing else. Search a word that will belong to only you and no one else, plus it should also satisfy your niche. You can also join two or more words to create your own terminology. That is advisable from me to you, **do this**. Because I did the same and trust me it works.

Your brand name could be joining the two known words and making one unique word that belongs to only your blog and no one else's. When you have a unique word that only belongs to you, then it is more than enough to rank number 1 and why? Simply because you don't have a rival yet.

Google is a giant search engine, so just imagine what will happen if a person searches a word and that word is only one in the world? Get the idea? You will be all over the first page.

You don't even have to worry about your SEO anymore regarding your name. Isn't that powerful? spend some nice time on the internet and according to you find or create terminology that will be unique.

I can say it proudly that because of this one step I got most of the views. Try it and you will be amazed. During the branding phase after you have created a good name for your brand, it is time to give it a LOGO.

## Making A Logo

This is absolutely an optional step. I myself don't have a logo for my blog but I recommend it to you. Making a logo that defines your brand could become an asset.

Think of it this way. If your blog shoots up and becomes the most popular around the globe then people will be able to recognize you just by your LOGO. And wherever your logo is present, will make an impact.

You can create your own logo in the comfort of your home. As a starter, try to do everything by yourself and do these steps so that whatever you come up with, will be connected to you in some way.

If you have no idea how to design a logo then you don't have to worry at all, you can hire a freelancer to do it for you for a very affordable price. Otherwise, you can even use free services like www.canva.com that helps you create picture-perfect icons and posters. But make sure that your brand name and logo stand out and leaves a statement.

Now you have your logo and brand name and I assume that you have used blogger.com to create your first blog. So now you should be familiar with every tab on the blogger dashboard.

Take time and learn everything by yourself. There are free tutorials on the internet that will explain to you every tab and what they do on www.blogger.com. It is actually really very easy then you think it is.

## Domain and Web-Hosting:

For this, you MUST spend a little bit of money to buy a domain and web hosting for your blog. I know it is a bit early, as you have just started making blogs but it is a crucial move.

www.blogger.com does provide you with a free URL domain but it no good and looks so unprofessional. When people see your blog, they should find a paid and nice-looking link which they can share with others. Since you have selected a unique terminology, getting a domain for that will be a piece of cake.

There are many softwares that provide domain and web hosting for a very affordable price such as

1. www.hostgator.com (highly recommended for web hosting)
2. www.bigrock.com (which I used for my blog)
3. www.godaddy.com (I have used it for my website)
4. www.bluehost.com (provide you with free SSL certificates)

There are million other platforms that provide the same services. Find them.

In case you don't know what domain and web-hosting are then let me tell you what it is in simple words. If you have visited any website then on the top you must have seen the URL right? Now that is a domain. www.yourbrandname.com is a domain and there are many more which you can choose from.

And for the web hosting, it is like a place where your brand resides (all your files are stored here). Say that you have a building and there is a name for that building. So, the name with be a domain and the building will be your web-hosting.

An area or place booked only for you. And yes, once you have a name sort out for your brand then make sure you have a business email for that particular name. You don't want people emailing you on your personal email, right?

So, you get it now that when people see a paid domain, they know that this guy is serious about his job.

And they can be safe that you are not spam or bot or something. That increases credibility.

When you have a:

1)Brand name

2)Logo (optional)

3)Domain

4)Web-hosting

It is time to go on blogger, WordPress, or anywhere else and create your blog.

Go to www.blogger.com and click on create a blog and just in a few minutes your blog will be ready. Then you can just make a few changes, install free templates, and play around to get a nice clean look. The same goes for WordPress as well.

The only difference is that to get WordPress, you have to first buy a domain and hosting and they provide you one-click WordPress installation.

# Chapter 5:

## *Design of The Blog*

*"The casual conversational tone of a blog is what makes it particularly dangerous"*

–Daniel Beaulieu

Once the blog is created it will look just like a standard web page with nothing to do as such. And trust me you don't want to post on that white sheet of the screen.

For that, you can go into the themes section and choose a template which best suits your brand. There are many free templates on blogger and WordPress which you can use and customize to look the best.

You can even download free templates from google and install them on your blog. It is easy too and you get different varieties. Obviously, you can choose a paid once also. What suits you?

Know this that people won't stay on your blog as long as the design is not attractive. Even if your content is "the best" you will lose a wide audience just because of that. I personally got myself a template from the internet and it looks much better. I keep changing just to try different things out. This is not advisable, try to find the best and stay with it for some time.

When you are customizing your template, make sure that everything is at the place and nothing is distorted. Your header, your blog name, title bar, main body, footer, and sidebar. All should be at the proper place.

Keep the follow button and comments on, so that you can get feedback frequently. One more thing, make sure that the template you are using is mobile friendly.

There are many templates that work with only desktops or laptops, and as we all know that most of the people around the world do most of their work from the mobile phone. So, if your blog is not mobile-friendly then you are losing.

Try to make it mobile-friendly or use themes that are mobile-friendly, so that people who are viewing it on mobile can also get a pleasing experience and they stay on their own will.

You may be thinking that it sounds like so much work. But trust me it is not that much at all. I started my blog in just one day, that's it. Just think of a niche, brand name and you are good to go.

Now in the header, you should include tabs like home page, about, contact, and social media if you have any with the same brand name. An 'about page' is very crucial because it tells people what your blog is about and they will decide if it bothers them or not.

Take time to craft the about page and keep it as true as possible. Choose words wisely and make a good about page that will force the reader to stay and follow you.

Just like the about page, the contact page is also very crucial. On this page, you will have your e-mail which you have created with the brand name, social media links, another website if you have any, and any other thing which you want to include.

Make sure to also insert a sign-up page which can keep track of the people who visited your blog and you will have data of their e-mails and I will tell you why these e-mails are important later.

# Chapter 6:

## *Your First Blog Post*

*"Don't try to plan everything out to the very last detail. I am a big believer in getting it out there: create a minimum viable product or website, launch it and get feedback"*

–Neil Patel

After you have all those things in place it is now time to publish your first blog post. Now this is very important as you may have heard that "The first impression is the last impression." Yes, it exists. Your first post has to be very good, which can catch attention.

### How to write the first post

Hmm. Now, this is interesting. You have done some research on your particular niche and you know what you want to write but still, don't go ahead and put everything rashly.

Take time, calm down, and then start writing. You certainly don't want to put the main information in your first post. When writing your first post, give it a suitable heading which is the most important thing and it must also have sub-headings.

Your first post must include who you are? In brief because in detail they can find in your 'about section'. Why you started this blog? What you have to offer? Why they must choose you and not some other and give a trailer of what you will be offering in your weekly posts.

Here your word art comes into play. Choose words which will attract people and make them believe that there is something in you that they must wait and see. If you could do that with your first post then you will surely win the war.

Use labels for every post of yours. It will make it easy to rank on the search engine. Once you have created your first post then make sure that you have everything in at the right place, see the demo of how it will look on your blog live, and then when satisfied – post it.

Know one thing about blogs is that you get the maximum number of views on the time you first post them. Try refreshing and see how much you get but don't get depressed if it shows only one or two. I have been there but I didn't get demotivated because I was writing my passion.

After you have set the post, you must go ahead and make accounts or pages on different social media platforms with the same brand name as your blog. This will bring in a new audience and more awareness. I recommend using pinterest.com (most of the people who love to read are available here), facebook.com, Instagram.com, Twitter, and whichever you are comfortable with. Initially PICK ONE!

**NOTE:** don't try to create your page on the first day on all the social media platforms. Build one by one.

First, you go to one media, have a bit of following there, and then go for the next one. You won't be able to handle all the platforms at once. You will know more about this as you upload more posts. Every post must be hand-crafted and chosen by you personally so that it can make a greater impact.

# Chapter 7:

## *Search Engine Optimization*

*"Readers subscribe to blogs when you provide an informational or entertainment value so great that it would be a loss to not subscribe to it"*

—Maki

To rank on the first page of Google, you need to keep these things into consideration, that not all the post you upload will rank on top just like that. This takes time. But yes, if you have a unique brand name and domain then you surely will rank on the top from the starting days just like I did.

Now for the SEO (Search Engine Optimization), I recommend you to use the webmaster tools. Once you have a blog going on, go ahead and submit it on the webmaster tool of Google which will help you index all your blog posts on Google search engine.

You can get all the statistics and data that you need about your blog from there. You can even request the search engine crawlers to crawl your blog on top and make it easy for people to search. That could be done for each and every post you upload and that is also going to give you credibility and exposure that you need.

SEO is not just about indexing your posts there are two types of SEO techniques namely: On-page SEO and Off-page SEO. Initially focus on the On-page which is using the right keywords in your blog post.

After selecting the topic, go ahead and make a search in the free google keyword planner tool which will give you a list of keywords that people are typing on the search bar. For your post to rank on the top, optimize your post with the keyword which most people are typing. Use those keywords multiple times in your blog post. Use only 3 keywords and use them in your heading, meta-data, and content. Beware, don't go overboard. Anything in excess is harmful.

The off-page technique is when you market your posts on social media and provide a link back to your post, you make an account on several other platforms that give you backlinks and do a lot of stuff to gain that initial traction. Combine both and you have a secret to success.

When done correctly, the right kind of people will come to your blog and you will get your audience. VOILA!! There is much-advanced stuff that is related to SEO but that has to be covered some other time.

## Chapter 8:

# *How to Monetize Your Blog?*

*"The first thing you need to decide when you build your blog is what you want to accomplish with it, and what it can do if successful"*

–Ron Dawson

There are again many ways in which you can monetize your blog. But don't do it until you have a decent amount of audience and a good view history every single day. I won't recommend you monetize your blog until you have a good number of views (minimum 2000-3000+ per day) and people following you. I have not monetized my blog yet.

But if you want you can do it, no harm. Let me give you some ways in which you can do that.

1) **Google Ads:**

Most of the people are looking for google ads. They want ads on their blogs. The way these ads work is that in a section somewhere in your blog post, there will be ads running continuously.

Now, whenever anyone comes to your blog and sees that ads and he likes the product and if he clicks, then you are paid. He buys or not that is a different issue but when he clicks you get paid. That is how ads work.

Now not just google ads, there are many softwares and companies that provide the ads in a similar fashion. The difference may be in the amount they pay you.

## 2)Sell your own product:

This could be a powerful way to earn money. You can sell your own products which you have developed say physical or any online course, books, etc. which you can offer to other people

This is safe and I say the fastest way to reach your money goals. The reason is that for all the product, the entire money will come to you or your company with no middle man. Hence more profit.

Say that your blog is on yoga, then your product could be yoga accessories like a yoga mat, shoes, clothes etc. That is how you start building your own company and eventually become a millionaire. [oops! Secret revealed]

## 3)Sell affiliate programs:

This could be another powerful way to keep money coming in. Affiliate means that you sell other people's products and whenever someone buys that product from your link you get paid a small commission of over that product, say 2, 3, 4, 10, 15% whatever. Isn't that amazing?

Now for an easy trick for the sake of earning more, you can use ads as well as affiliate and you can sell your own products. Meaning you can combine two or all of the above ways and earn more money. Highly recommended.

For this, the signup forms on your blog will come handy. Whoever signs up, readily says that they are interested in your content. You can add them on your email list funnel and slowly and gradually you will have a huge email list.

You can then send them emails once every alternate day or every week, depends on you, regarding your product of course and if they buy, you get profit. That is called EMAIL MARKETING.

There is a saying that **"money is in the list"** that is so true. You have access to people who like your content, what else do you want? Sell them your products and earn your fortune.

# Chapter 9:

## *How to Get 50K+ Views*

*"Blogging is hard because of the grind required to stay interesting and relevant"*

–Sufia Tippu

Now it is time to get 50K+ views, are you ready? Let's get started. Let me be clear here that reaching 50,000 views on your first blog is not a simple task. There are many things that come into consideration. You could commit many mistakes that could cost you everything or you can even become a millionaire. Depends on you!

It is all in the mind. The more you believe and do and provide the more you get back. For getting 50K views you need one thing and one thing only, you know what? Can you guess? Yes, right you need "VIEWERS" It is simple, you need people who can view your content and like it. For that, you need to have a positive exposure.

For starters say that you have a unique brand name and because of that you are getting a few views. But you cannot remain at the same level, can you? You must level up. For going a level higher, you create social media following, which means you put some of your content on your social media and say that for the remaining information, click the link, and just like that, they are on your blog.

Let me tell you a secret, don't tell it to anyone okay, THE SECRET IS THAT "there is no limit on how many posts you publish per day" Shhh!!!...

So, don't just sit there saying that you have made that one post, or one tweet. Do as much as you can, make your post reach your target audience.

SECRET 2: Find other bloggers just with the same niche as you and collaborate with them to make content. Here you get a ready-made audience without doing anything. Now his audience will know you and if they like what you deliver, they will end up on your blog as well.

The key element here is to SHARE…

Share your blog to as many places as you can. Run ads, post, the tweet goes all out and eventually you will reach 50,000 views and you can go higher as well.

The rest is up to you. Don't quit in the middle of a sea, reach on an island of jewels. If you start then see it through. I had only 10 views in my first whole month, but eventually, by the end of 8th month, I got 50K views.

Congratulations on finishing the book and GOOD LUCK for what awaits next.

# Chapter 10:

# *A Quick Story*

*"Share your story, write your passion and enjoy every step of the way. You are born to change lives"*

—Ahemad R Kazi

When I started my first blog, I was passionate to write about my favorite dream car – ROLLS ROYCE. I could talk about it for many hours and still be interested in that. All of my friends know that I am a big fan of Rolls Royce.

I even had an advantage that I knew everything about Rolls Royce cars like all its models, its story, its history, its upcoming model and its features and characteristics. I didn't have to learn about any of that. So, I just started writing whenever I was free.

There was one more thing, I didn't start that Blog because I was interested in Rolls Royce. No! I started because I know that most of the people are interested in the 'WORLD'S MOST EXPENSIVE CARS' as well.

Rolls Royce has a very distinctive look and amazing features which made it stand out from the crowd immediately. That is when I started writing my blog. I was not a great writer but yeah, I was passionate. I never did start for money or to be true I didn't know back then that I could earn money from it.

It was a month later that I discovered we could even earn money from it. I was committed to one post per week. Every fine Sunday I used to get up and post **at the same time**. Sometimes, I used to write the post beforehand and schedule it on Sunday to publish automatically.

It was just a fun gig for me. One month passed and I got no more than 10 views (including my family). It was horrible. In the next month, I got almost 50 views, a little better but still terrible.

But who needed views anyway? I just kept on writing and my views increased from 50 to 100 to a 1000. I was so much happy when I saw the first 1000 views on my blog. I thought that I was a champion. I saw the analytics and I realized that I was getting views from 10 different countries.

Slowly I created a Facebook page of my blog for promotion purpose. After that, I went for Pinterest because I know that people come here to read specifically. I created there a business profile and boom when I promoted on these two platforms, I was getting monthly 1000 views. Could you imagine?

Slowly and gradually my number of views increased and every month was better than all the previous months combined. It was a big achievement for me. As time passed, my viewers increased and my blog was viewed in so many different countries. The countries I never heard of were viewing my content. The countries which were seeing my blog were as follows.

United States, India, Germany, Belgium, Ukraine, Russia, the United Kingdom, Peru, China, Hong Kong,

Indonesia, Spain, Norway, Kuwait, UAE, Sri Lanka, Abu Dhabi, Italy, Philippines, Israel, Finland, South Africa, France, Ireland, Canada, Cameroon, Malaysia, Australia, Singapore, Pakistan, Cyprus, Kenya, Yemen, Bangladesh, New Zealand, Nepal, Slovakia, Turkey, Ghana, Barbados, Qatar, Poland, Angola, Romania, Greece etc.

Around a total of 45 countries. It was amazing. I didn't know something like this was even possible. And it was only 7 months until I got my first 50,002 views. The feeling was amazing and it was an awesome journey as well.

I hope that you will achieve something like this and better as well. GOOD LUCK!!!

P.S: After writing my first blog I became self-aware that I could do something more with my writing skills. That is when I took time off and started all over again. I now have a dream of inspiring **10 million people** worldwide to take massive action. To accomplish my dreams, I created a new blog to help you attain your wildest dreams. You can check it out now, it's called >> www.gemstorycreator.com <<

# Conclusion

There is one advice I wish to pass on before I leave and that is: whatever you do, don't stay mediocre. Because it hurts more than failing. Choose to die while fighting rather than dying without doing anything.

This blog is usually a start to every person who has the mindset of an entrepreneur. After the blog, there are many things that you will start and scale.

So, don't give up after your first attempt. Hope you have gained some value from this book. If yes then go ahead and apply it. Knowledge without application is just a recycle bin. Use it to your fullest extent and make something happen.

I leave you with that thought and hope that you will utilize what you have learned in the most profitable way there is. UNTIL NEXT TIME...

**NOTE:** If you like this book then do share it with your friends and leave a review on amazon. That will surely help me and many others who are looking to purchase this book.

Besides this, I have a series going on called "SUCCESSFUL DREAM" make sure to get it as well from amazon. The books are awesome, and in the first 2 months I sold the first book to 150 people internationally and you won't believe that each and every single person loved it.

# *"My Latest Book"*

<u>**The Inheritance of Dreams**</u>: Effective Business Strategies and Life Principles Through Storytelling

## Synopsis:

Your true success, wealth, and happiness are three generations away. All three are here to help you attain your success. The Inheritance of Dreams is a unique combination of thrilling dialogues, precious business and life lessons, money-making laws, family emotions, incredible instances, heart-breaking love, infinite motivation, an entertaining story package, and many soul-shaking aphorisms.

It begins with our hero Cooper, a 17-year-old middle-class family boy, who accidentally stumbles upon something ravishing and eye-catching, which he loves the most for the first time but cannot owe it just because he is not RICH.

He vows to own that beauty with his full heart and pure complete determination. He gets surrounded by adversities and failures but never wavers. He shatters his limits and goes beyond by increasing his assets and skillsets and tries to build a FORTUNE for himself.

Coming along, you will also encounter a man possessing a special gift who challenges time to become a millionaire. The ironic chemistry between a broken billionaire and an abandoned orphan named King will leave you stunned and smiling.

Will they achieve their absolute dreams? Let's find out together.

**Available on Amazon – Get it Now! You will be glad you did!**